BRIT
ICE HOCKE
FROM THE G

G000078484

With Commentary

By: Trevor Boyce

Published by:
Yore Publications
12 The Furrows, Harefield,
Middx. UB9 6AT.

© Trevor Boyce 1997

....

British Library Cataloguing-in-Publication Data.
A catalogue record for this book
is available from the British Library.

ISBN 1 874427 12 7

YORE PUBLICATIONS normally specialise in football
(soccer) books of an historical nature, including club
histories. Three free newsletters are issued per year,
for your first copy send a S.A.E. (Ref. H) to:

Yore Publications, 12 The Furrows,
Harefield, Middx. UB9 6AT, England.

Printed and bound by The Book Factory

Acknowledgements

The Complete Book of the Olympics   David Wallechinsky
Flashing Blades   Phil Drackett
The Herald Ice Hockey Annual   Bernards Stocks
The History of Middlesex C.C.C.   Daid Lemmon
The Ice Hockey Annual
(Formerly The Ice Hockey Newsletter Annual)   Stewart Roberts
Ice Hockey Fan
Ice Hockey Herald
Ice Hockey- the International Game   Robert Giddens
Ice Hockey Newsletter
Ice Hockey News Review
Ice Hockey World
Ice Hockey World Annual   Robert Giddens/Phil Drackett
Ice Hockey Yearbook   Gordon Wade
The I.I.H.F. Yearbook
Nottingham Panthers-a Pictorial History
100 Years of Hockey in Manitoba   Vince Leah
The Puck Chasers of Manchester
Puck Magazine
Skating   Capt Duff Taylor
The Southern Ice Hockey Association Yearbook
Speedway Star
Vendetta on Ice   Phil Drackett

The above mentioned publications have all been of assistance in some part to the compilation of this book, as have contributions of, recollections, and/or memorabilia from Martin Harris, Phil Drackett, Pete Wickham and Tony Barnwell, and the official programmes from Wembley, Harringay, Earls Court, Streatham, Nottingham, Slough and Brighton.

The quality of the reproduction of photographs is not always as would have been desired, but the difficulty in obtaining originals resulted in the necessity of using copies. Every effort was made to trace the source of photographs but in view of the age of many, this was not always possible, therefore the author offers his apologies should copyright have inadvertently been infringed or an acknowledgment not given.

CONTENTS:

Introduction

I was seventeen years old before I went to my first ice hockey game. Until that time I lived for football alone. If I was not playing for my school or local team, I was kicking a ball around in the park, and if I was not kicking a ball around, I was reading a soccer magazine or programme - except for Saturday afternoons that is, when you could find me with the rest of my family at that mecca of association football, Griffin Park, the home of Brentford Football Club.

The 1965/66 football season had been over for a month or more and I was pretty bored. England's first game in the historic World Cup was just 30 days away, but I was looking for something to do, particularly as it was a Saturday evening.

A small column caught my eye in the London Evening News. Wembley Lions were playing Brighton Tigers in an ice hockey game at the Empire Pool, Wembley. I had watched the odd game of ice hockey on TV and had also heard of these two famous old teams, but went along with an open mind - just looking for a nights entertainment that would help me to get by until my next fix of soccer.

What I saw that night changed me for ever. I still love football, I still love Brentford, but I was transfixed by the speed, skill, colour, grace and hurly-burly of ice hockey. Everything seemed to gel together to make a special evening of atmosphere and entertainment. The organ music, drums beating, horns hooting and the fans chanting in this packed old arena which simply oozed tradition, while the two teams of gladiators fought out for the ultimate accolade.

What I didn't realise that night was the parlous state British ice hockey was in. The National League had collapsed six years earlier, and the few teams that had survived until 1966 played only challenge matches or home tournaments. Despite the Lions attracting near full houses at the Empire Pool, most clubs were attracting the proverbial "one man and his dog", and Brighton - the other famous club participating that particular evening did not even have a home rink, just coming together for the odd game to give Wembley some attractive opposition.

The Lions themselves were afforded little ice time, filling vacant Saturday's between the ice shows and other sporting events. The team, stocked with ageing National League stars folded half-way through the 1968/69 season.

The programme editorial for their last game at the Empire Pool against Paisley Mohawks on November 30th included: "Exciting prospect in store for Wembley fans is the possibility of a match between Lions and a team representing the Canadian Services in Europe here next Spring." The match never took place. Lions beat Paisley 3-0 in a penalty-ridden game, and two weeks later travelled to Whitley Bay to record a 6-1 victory in their last ever game.

It took many years and a lot of hard work from a devoted few to put the game back on the British map, but I have never doubted that ice hockey could and should be a major sport in this country. Only time will tell if the Super League will bring in a new golden age, but a team in London - preferably at Wembley - will not do the competition any harm.

Present day hockey fans may not realise that in the North American scene of the 1930's, only 8 to 10 teams competed in the NHL as opposed to 26 these days. Many of the players who did not quite make the grade came to England to play in the ENL, which was considered as good as any standard outside the NHL.

Although I missed the 'golden days' I have always been interested in that era of the British game, and when Warren Rost asked me to write a page in the Slough Jets matchday programme with his Grandad Sonny, I jumped at the chance. I could dig out the facts and figures while Sonny could provide the anecdotes'.

This book is a compilation of some of the best of those articles, and not meant to be a chronological history of the British game. Hopefully however, it will revive happy memories to some older fans, while providing an insight of the early days to the present generation of supporters.

Trevor Boyce

The Road to the Golden Years

There is enough evidence to suggest that ice hockey has been played in Britain - in one form or another - for hundreds of years, and maybe even longer. It was played on the frozen fens of East Anglia during medieval times, while in 1855 the 'Illustrated London News' published a drawing of gentlemen in top hats chasing a ball with sticks in their hands on the frozen River Thames at Richmond.

The first artificial ice rinks were opened in this country in 1876. Two were in London - both called the Glacarium. The first was at Charing Cross and the second just a few miles away in the King's Road, Chelsea. Manchester also housed one at Rusholme, but it closed within twelve months due to the "inelastic characteristic of its surface and intense cold." The rinks were popular with skaters but did not automatically take on ice hockey, and the first recorded match between two British teams was not until 1885 when Oxford University beat their counterparts from Cambridge, 6-0, at St. Moritz in Switzerland - though some pundits believe this game to have been bandy, not ice hockey.

Despite another rink opening near to St. James's Park in London, ice hockey was generally restricted at this time to those who could afford winter jaunts to the Alps. This finally changed when the Prince's Club installed a rink at their headquarters behind Harrods in Knightsbridge. Prince's was an exclusive sporting club, and in the 1870's was the home of Middlesex Cricket Club before they moved to Lord's. On one side of the ground "society forgathered and practised roller-skating, which was in vogue just then." One assumes that the members eventually progressed from roller to ice skating, and in 1897 Major B.M. Patton was given permission by the founder of Prince's Skating Club, Admiral Maxe, to form an ice hockey team.

In 1895, on the site of which is now the London Palladium, the National Skating Club had built a rink which was known as Hengler's. Two ice hockey teams were based at the rink - Argyll and the Amateur Skating Club (sometimes known as Hengler's) - and in 1903, with three from the Knightsbridge rink, Prince's, Cambridge University and London Canadians, they formed the first English League which was won by Canadians who only dropped two points in the eight game schedule - two more than Prince's. The League folded after two seasons and Hengler's closed in 1909. Prince's also stopped hosting ice hockey, and for a while after the Great War only a rink at Cheetham Hill in Manchester, which opened in

1910, was featuring the sport in England. There were several English clubs still playing - mainly based at the Universities or in the armed forces - but they played nearly all their games on the continent until a new rink was opened in 1926 at Westminster.

A Southern League was partially completed in the 1929/30 season, but a turning point for English hockey was the formation of a team who played at the Grosvenor House Hotel, Park Lane, in London. The Grosvenor House Canadians were generally regarded as the first team to play for 'expenses' and made their debut in the 1931/32 English League. Canadians finished the campaign in fourth place behind Champions Oxford University, and runners-up London Lions plus a combined Prince's & Queen's team. Below them were Manchester, Sussex and Cambridge University.

The Oxford varsity team played out of the original rink built in the city, which was later to be converted to a cinema, while Cambridge played at the recently opened Streatham rink. London Lions played at Hammersmith in a building that would soon become the famous Palais, while Sussex played in Hove and Prince's and Queen's played in Bayswater where the Queen's rink is still located today. The 'Dark Blues' won the title again in 1932/33 with Canadians in second place and Lions in third, followed by Prince's & Queen's, Cambridge and Manchester, Sussex having dropped out of the league. Grosvenor House took the Championship at their third - and last - attempt in 1933/34 followed by Queen's and Oxford University.

The newly formed Streatham and Warwickshire (Birmingham) teams finished in mid-table positions in front of Manchester and Cambridge. London Lions had folded as their rink was converted to a dance hall and their ice plant moved to Richmond.

The 1934/35 season can considered as the start of the golden era. The Empire Pool had opened at Wembley and they decided to run with two teams. The Grosvenor House rink had closed down and was converted to a banqueting hall, so the nucleus of the squad moved across London to become Wembley Canadians. The other team to play at the 10,000 seater arena revived another popular name and became Wembley Lions. They finished second and third respectively behind Streatham, with another new team in fourth place - Richmond Hawks. Behind Richmond were Warwickshire, Manchester and Oxford University, but the days of the smaller rinks were numbered. Queen's, Oxford University, Warwickshire and Manchester all declined to enter the league competition in season 1935/36, finding it difficult to compete with the other clubs who were moving away from the amateur status of previous years. This was partially offset by three teams joining the competition and playing at two new and exciting venues. Two were to play at the 7,000 seat arena erected in the exhibition grounds at Earls Court, and another at a new rink in Brighton which housed 3,000. The new teams - Earls Court Rangers, Brighton Tigers, and Kensington Corinthians, all found the going tough against the established teams and finished fifth, sixth and seventh respectively. The Championship was won by Wembley Lions who pipped Richmond Hawks on goal average, while Streatham had to settle for third place - despite being just one point behind. Canadians slipped two places from the previous year, finishing in fourth position.

1936/37 was another big year for the English National League, and four new teams ensured that a 40 game schedule could be played in the main tournament. Two teams came from the new 8,220 seat arena at Harringay in North London, while the other two came from Paris, France. Kensington Corinthians - who had finished bottom of the 1935/36 campaign attempted to lose their 'Cinderella' image by changing their name to Earls Court Royals, while at the Empire Pool, Canadians opted for the more patriotic Wembley Monarchs. The French Clubs, Paris Rapides and Français Volantes, were liberally stocked with French-Canadians who added excitement and colour to the fast-growing sport. However the franc was devalued, and it was soon evident that their participation was not viable due to the cost of running the teams and the difficulties of transportation.

A quick reorganisation was needed, and it was agreed that the teams would be relocated in England. Southampton, which had opened in 1931, took the place of Français Volantes, and because their jerseys depicted a 'V' they opted for the name Southampton Vikings. Manchester had applied to rejoin the League at the start of the season, but had been turned down by the British Ice Hockey Association because the rink capacity and ice surface were both too small. Despite competition from Liverpool and Birmingham, they were this time elected to the League as Manchester Rapids.

Lions took the League title for the second consecutive year with the two Harringay teams - Racers and Greyhounds - in second and third place. Richmond Hawks had lost their coach, Percy Nicklin, and nucleus of players to Harringay and finished with the wooden spoon. Hawks never recovered from this setback, and with Manchester and Southampton - who were also playing in ice rinks rather than arenas - decided not to compete at the top level in 1937/38. Earls Court Royals found that their name change did not improve attendances, and the Empress Hall decided to go with one team the Rangers.

8

The League went back to a 24 game schedule, but this did not stop Harringay Racers from winning it by a record thirteen points. The rest of the teams fought a close contest, and only seven points separated second place Wembley Monarchs and bottom club Streatham. The same seven teams started season 1938/39 but, after being found guilty of disciplinary and administrative irregularities, Streatham were thrown out of the League. Racers conceded the League title to their stable-mates Harringay Greyhounds, who pipped Wembley Lions to the championship by one point.

With the outbreak of World War Two, many of the players either stayed in Canada or were conscripted to the armed forces and, as with other sports, it appeared that league competition for 1939/40 may have to be suspended. The Harringay teams had access to more players than the others clubs, and offered to share them. Eventually a five team league was organised, the two teams from Harringay competing with their North London rivals from Wembley and the reinstated Streatham. Greyhounds held on to their championship title with Racers in second place, who were followed by Monarchs, Lions and Streatham respectively.

The English National League was then held over for six years - until season 1946/47. The five teams from the last competition were joined by Brighton Tigers and a new club - Nottingham Panthers. The 3,000 seat Nottingham Ice Stadium had opened at the outset of hostilities, but had to wait until November 1946 before they could introduce the Panthers to the public. Panthers finished bottom with only seven wins from 36 games while Brighton won their first League championship trophy.

With the same seven teams competing in 1947/48, Tigers won the championship again much to the surprise of many pundits who considered the side to be "over the hill." The League expanded the following year when, for the first time in almost a decade, Earls Court Rangers took part in the ENL. They struggled all year and only Wembley Lions finished below them. Harringay Racers won the championship title for the second time - 11 points clear of second place Streatham.

As with many sports, the fans had flocked back to ice hockey after the war, but the golden days were in fact numbered. The country was in a recession and the sport began a slow process of decline. The emergence of television and the Entertainment Tax meant that the large arenas had to diversify to break even. In season 1949/50, Harringay decided to cut twice ENL winners, Harringay Greyhounds. The smaller rinks were also struggling to meet overheads and the schedule of the Autumn Cup was increased to 36 games in order to help them survive. This meant that Wembley, the only rink to support two clubs, was sometimes hosting hockey on three consecutive nights. This was obviously not financially viable and the National League went back to a 24 game schedule.

The arenas also started to split the season, having a two to three month break over Christmas to host circuses, ice shows and, in later years, gospel crusades. Despite the cut-backs it was rumoured that some star players were earning as much as £25 a week - a small fortune in 1949. Yet it was Streatham, one of the lowest paid teams in the League that won the 1949/50 League title.

Sadly - and almost inevitably - Wembley dropped a team for the 1950/51 campaign. They cut the Monarchs despite the fact that they finished two places above the Lions the previous year. Nottingham Panthers finished bottom of the pile in the Autumn Cup, and amazed everyone by winning their first League championship, one point clear of Brighton.

The same six teams competed once again in both 1951/52 and 1952/53. Lions won their first post-war championship in 1951/52, three points clears of Earls Court Rangers who were enjoying their most successful of nine ENL campaigns, while Streatham won the following year - five points ahead of Harringay Racers.

The ENL was reduced to five teams in 1953/54 when Earls Court Rangers- who could never emulate the crowds or success of the Wembley and Harringay clubs - dropped out of the League. In March 1954 Harringay were also to lose their home - to the Billy Graham Greater London Crusade - and Racers were forced to play their last seven 'home' games at Earls Court. Nottingham Panthers won their second League title by a single point from Streatham. It was clear that a revamp was needed. With only five teams in the ENL there was not enough variety of competition, and for several years the promoters had been looking enviously North across the border at the thriving Scottish League. In the early days of the English 'golden era', ice hockey in Scotland had been played almost exclusively at Crossmyloof in Glasgow, but in 1936/37 Perth Panthers joined the Scottish National League.

The Central Scotland Ice Rink had a capacity of 3,100 and - as the sport proved popular - a number of other mini-stadia were built to house ice hockey. Kirkcaldy (4,000), Dundee (3,665), Falkirk (4,500), Ayr (3,800) and Dunfermline (3,400) all joined the League, before the war stopped regular competition.

Paisley and Murrayfield, both 4,500 capacity, had also opened but, as with Nottingham, had to wait until the end of hostilities to participate in league action.

In 1954/55 it was hoped that the eight teams from Scotland and five from England would provide enough variety of competition in the new British National League to excite the most discerning of hockey fans. Unfortunately problems were encountered right from the start, and Streatham decided not to enter - citing the fact that the extra travelling would cost them another £100 a week.

A twelve team, 22 game Autumn Cup schedule was won by Harringay Racers, followed by Falkirk Lions and Paisley Pirates. Dunfermline Vikings could only muster two victories and it was no surprise when 11 games into the National League programme they folded and their record expunged. Racers also won the inaugural League championship, but in the summer there was more bad news when all the Scottish clubs except Paisley Pirates decided they could not afford to promote senior ice hockey.

In season 1955/56 - in only its second year - the British National League was reduced to five teams. Nottingham Panthers won the championship from Wembley Lions by the smallest of margins when they both finished with 35 points from 32 games. Cellar club Racers were only 8 points adrift in a close and exciting competition. The same five teams contested 1956/57 and 1957/58, which were won by Wembley Lions and Brighton Tigers respectively. Lack of domestic opposition was now enhanced by the visit of many overseas teams, while the British clubs, forced out of their homes by ice shows and their like, undertook extensive European tours. A landmark on October 31st 1957 was Sonny Rost's 1,000th appearance for a Wembley team.

The season 1957/58 will be remembered as the last at Harringay - the arena closed to become a supermarket warehouse. Racers last game was on 26th April when they beat Paisley Pirates 10-4. The programme notes stated that ice hockey was as popular as ever, and that the re-entry of Streatham would be a fillip. Ironically, neither team appeared the following season.

The closure meant that there was only four teams left to compete in the 1958/59 British National League, but the cavalry arrived in the form of Edinburgh Royals who entered the Autumn Cup, providing Paisley with a 'derby' game. Despite finishing as runners-up to Brighton, they were reported to be losing £200 a week and elected not to compete in the League proper. The four team 30 game schedule was won for the first time by Paisley Pirates.

The 1959/60 season again brought optimism as Streatham rejoined the circuit after a five year absence. However, their return only delayed the inevitable. Harringay and Earls Court were no longer operating, while Wembley Lions were homeless for a large part of the season and there were rumours at Brighton that the new owners of the Sports Stadium were not interested in promoting ice hockey.

The 'new boys' from South London won both the League Championship and Autumn Cup, while Brighton were the first play-off trophy winners in thirty years, beating Nottingham Panthers 6-5 on aggregate after a dramatic overtime period.

At the British Ice Hockey Association AGM, Nottingham director Phil Walker was quoted as saying, "It is extremely doubtful that senior hockey will operate next season." Despite a successful year, Streatham's owner - William Warner scratched them from the League. Wembley and Nottingham were not interested in reverting to a four team competition, and the first British League folded.

British ice hockey was to be left out in the cold for many years, and it was not until the early 1980's that a National League competition was revived, but that is another story........

English & British National League Champions 1934/35 to 1959/60

English National League
1934/35: Streatham
1935/36: Wembley Lions
1936/37: Wembley Lions
1937/38: Harringay Racers
1938/39: Harringay Greyhounds
1939/40: Harringay Greyhounds
1946/47: Brighton Tigers
1947/48: Brighton Tigers
1948/49: Harringay Racers
1949/50: Streatham
1950/51: Nottingham Panthers
1951/52: Wembley Lions
1952/53: Streatham
1953/54: Nottingham Panthers

British National League
1954/55: Harringay Racers
1955/56: Nottingham Panthers
1956/57: Wembley Lions
1957/58: Brighton Tigers
1958/59: Paisley Pirates
1959/60: Streatham

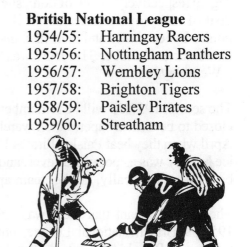

I'll Take Hockey Any Time

I'm a fairly peaceful man, an old time baseball fan,
You can hear me yell when Heilman hits the ball;
And I howl when Ty Cobb stabs one, and I growl when Speaker
grabs one,
And I roar when Babe Ruth's homer hits the wall.
But the Diamond sport is quiet to that reeling rousing riot,
To a slashing game of hockey at its prime;
It's a shindig wild and gay, it's a battle served frappé;
Give me hockey, I'll take hockey any time!

Once while crazy with the heat, I coughed up to buy a seat,
Just to see a pair of robbers grab a purse,
It was a cinch and stall and shove, and "Please excuse my glove",
Till I blessed them with a healthy Irish curse,
But for fighting fast and free, grab your hat and come with me
Sure the thing they call boring is a crime,
And for ground and lofty whacking and enthusiastic smacking,
Give me hockey, I'll take hockey any time!

I've an ever ready ear for a rousing football cheer,
And I love to see a half-back tackle low,
It's a really gorgeous sight when the boys begin to fight
With a touchdown only half a yard to go,
But take all the most exciting parts of football baseball fighting,
And mix them up to make a game sublime,
Serve it up with lots of ice, you don't have to ask me twice,
Give me hockey, I'll take hockey any time!

Yes for speed and pep and action, there is only one attraction,
You'll see knockouts there - a dozen for a dime,
When the bright steel blades are ringing, and the shinny sticks
are swinging,
Give me hockey, I'll take hockey any time!

Anon.

❀ ❀ ❀ ❀ ❀ ❀ ❀ ❀ ❀ ❀ ❀ ❀ ❀ ❀ ❀ ❀ ❀

(From a 1950 programme for a game between Waterloo Hurricanes and
Windsor Spitfires of the Ontario Hockey Association)

No 1: Sonny Rost, Wally Monson & Bert Peer.

Sonny Rost

In 1934, at the age of 21, Sonny Rost travelled from Winnipeg to London to play at the recently opened Empire Pool & Sports Arena in Wembley. He was still playing when the National League collapsed in 1960, and had been inducted to the Hockey Hall of Fame in 1955 along with Wally Monson and Bert Peer.

Sonny came over originally to play for Wembley Canadians, but over the years he played for all the great Wembley teams, and in 1955 he reminisced that for half his life he had been happy and proud to wear a Wembley uniform.

The 1955/56 'Ice Hockey World Annual' recorded the three new admissions thus:

Sonny Rost has a record without parallel in the annals of senior hockey. He was a Wembley player when the rink first opened in 1934, he was a Wembley player in 1955, 21 years later.

He has coached and played with both Monarchs and Lions and probably his most notable achievement was in leading the former to the Autumn Cup and International Tournament titles in 1948/49. The following year Monarchs were runners-up in the League, Autumn Cup and National Tournament.

Wally Monson. Known variously as 'Pop' or 'Foxy', baldheaded centre-ice Walter Monson was captain of Harringay Racers from their formation in 1936 until the end of the 1939/40 season. Racers were League Champions in 1937/38 and runners-up on two other occasions.

Since retiring Monson has coached Winnipeg Monarchs, crack Canadian junior team, and has been the means of recruiting many players for English hockey, notably Milt Swindlehurst, George Tamblyn, Mike Daski, Ron Barr, Bruce Bell, Laurie Mitchell and Gord Fashaway.

Wally Monson

Bert Peer

Bert Peer. Possibly the greatest right-winger in the history of senior amateur hockey, giant Bert Peer made a remarkable impact during the years he played with Harringay.

His best year was his first (1936) when he placed third in the scoring to Johnny Acheson and Don Willson and was voted to the 'World' All-Star 'A' team. He later played professional hockey in the United States and American Hockey Leagues. If he had taken his hockey more seriously there is no doubt he would have made the NHL.

From Sonny ......

Best pal-Jake Milford

Clarence Victor Rost
I left Winnipeg in September 1934 with Jake Milford, my best pal, who later became the General Manager of the Vancouver Canucks. He was also a member of the Hall of Fame, but sadly has passed away.

It took 2½ days to travel to Montreal, and then 14 days on the 'Ascania Liner'. We were met at Tilbury by Stadium Manager Paul Herbert in his bright red sports car, who seemed to us to be a mad man behind the wheel- driving on the wrong (!) side of the road.

Arriving to find Wembley Arena (In those days known as the Empire Pool) not finished, we got down to a bit of labouring. I joined Wembley Canadians who had previously competed as Grosvenor House Canadians, and whose rink had been on the top floor of the Hotel in Park Lane, London. They were watched by Lords and Ladies in penguin suits.

The Empire Pool, Wembley.... as it looked in 1934.

Wembley was the best days of my life, except for my wife Marge and my three hockey mad children.

Wally Monson
Wally was from Winnipeg, and was bald by the age of 25 - which earned him the nickname 'Pop'. He was one of the best centerman in the game with slide rule passing and a "try and get the puck off me" attitude. He was a team leader who had the respect of all the players.

Bert Peer
If Bert had taken the game seriously, he would have been in the NHL's 'Big Six'. A big, strong, player, he was a forward to be feared by all. He was a little greedy with the puck but could split a defence as if he had an axe in his hands. Not the best team man in the world, but who is perfect?

No. 2: Anning/Kauppi/Steele - The 'Kid' Line

Sonny Rost has been quoted as saying that he enjoyed best the years he played with Wembley Monarchs. After the war Monarchs had several talented squads which peaked in 1948/49 when they won the Autumn Cup and the International Tournament. In 1946/47- the first competitive year after the war - they had to settle for runners-up in the Autumn Cup. A March 1947 edition of 'Ice Hockey World' led with this article on their famous 'Kid' Line:

"The individual scoring race looks a sure thing for Bobby Lee, but the joust for the honour of being the highest-scoring line is still on. Strongest end of schedule bid comes from Monarchs 'Kid' Line of Les Anning, Mauno Kauppi, and George Steele. To date Kauppi, the kid from Barrie has 49 points, Steele 46, while Anning leads the way with 52.

"To take the honours they have seven other high-pressure lines to contend with, all with over 100 points in the regular league schedule. Tops at the moment are Harringay Racers first line of 'Ken' Kennedy flanked by the Fashaway brothers, Joe and Cordie.

"This line aggregate is 170. That means the 'Kids' have something to beat, but a line that musn't be overlooked is that the Monarchs trio have been garnering points 'ad lib' in the last few games, the nonce Racers triumvirate have been held practically scoreless."

From Sonny......

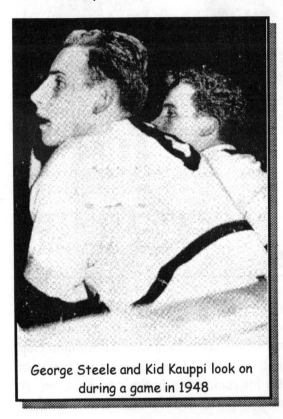

George Steele and Kid Kauppi look on during a game in 1948

Kauppi, Anning and Steele arrived at Wembley and were awestruck at the size of the rink. Still a little seasick they went straight into a game and the 'Greenhorn' line was formed. A few weeks later they were renamed the 'Kid' line, making an immediate impact. A very dangerous combination,

Les Anning in 1947

high scoring - but more importantly giving the fans value for money with their fast skating and passing. Anning was the fastest player I have ever seen in British ice hockey. Kauppi was a great stickhandler, playmaker and rough when things reached boiling point. Steele was a tireless backchecker, and a real team man.

The line of Kennedy and the Fashaway brothers was a coaches dream. Gordie Fashaway was a big danger man and scored goals from anywhere on the ice. Putting a 'tag' on Gordie would slow down the line considerably as the opposition found.

No 3: Archie Stinchcombe

Many newcomers to British ice hockey may be amazed to learn that Britain was once the Olympic Champions. In 1936 Great Britain won the Gold Medal in the German Alps at Garmisch-Partenkirchen, the first time that Canada had failed to win. There was much controversy about the validity of some of the British players, several of whom (as in the modern national squad) had Canadian accents!

One of these medalists was left-wing Archie Stinchcombe. Archie was born on 17th November 1912 at Cudworth, near Barnsley in Yorkshire, but spent his childhood in Ontario, Canada. He played with the Ontario Hockey Association Champions, Windsor Mic-Macs, and later with Falconbridge Miners.

Because he lost an eye in an accident, NHL rules barred him from progress in that direction and he came to England in 1935 to play for Streatham. Three seasons later he moved to Wembley Lions and then went to stable-mates Monarchs for a year.

After the war he returned to Streatham, before finishing his career as player-coach and then coach of Nottingham Panthers. It was at his home - still in Nottingham - that he sadly died on 3rd November 1994.

In 1988 he attended a Gold Medal Winners reception at Buckingham Palace where it was reported that the Princess Royal was *"amused and interested with his vivid recollections of that 1936 triumph."* He once said that the reason he went to Wembley was that it meant, *"no more going into the corners with 'Postie' (Sonny Rost)."*

19

From Sonny......

Archie Stinchcombe played most of his hockey at Streatham with Harvey 'Red' Stapleford, George Shaw, Gerry Davey (Olympic team), and Carl Erhardt, who did a great deal for the game in Britain. Archie had one of the hardest shots in the game - which came from his strong wrists - and he could shoot in full stride.

Claim to fame: While earning his Olympic medal he had his passport signed by Adolf Hitler.

His favourite Story: While playing golf in Nottingham, he suffered a less than fatal heart attack and was carried by club members to a sofa. A very efficient young steward came over and told him to take his shoes off as he was getting mud on the sofa! "Never mind about me" cried Archie.

He married Gwen - a figure skater from Streatham - and they were inseparable until his death. I (Sonny) was there at his funeral to see him off to the big ice rink in the sky.

No 4: Chick Zamick

21 year old Victor 'Chick' Zamick arrived in Nottingham in 1947 as a late replacement for the Panthers with £30 in his pocket and a suit borrowed from his brother. With his slight appearance, the pundits of that day did not believe that he would be a success but they were soon proven wrong as he smashed record after record in an eleven year spell with the midland outfit.

Elected to the Hall of Fame as early as 1951 his citation read "Zamick's meteorical progress in English hockey needs no repeating here. Suffice to say that he is one of only two players to score over 300 goals." In fact he went on to be the first player to score 1,000 goals in a career that ended at Wembley after a spell as player-coach in Switzerland with Servette.

Chick's debut for the Lions was a London Tournament game against Brighton Tigers in October 1963 where he scored two goals in a 5-4 victory. The programme noted that *"Winnipeg-born Zamick, the kingpin at Nottingham from 1947-58, has won the admiration of ice fans everywhere."*

Playing for Brighton was John Rost, and the programme also went on to record that, *"voted 'Most Promising Young Player' at Brighton at the end of last season was 19 year-old right-winger, John Rost, son of former*

Wembley star, Sonny Rost. John certainly seems to be following in his dad's footsteps as far as playing exciting hockey is concerned." The same could now, of course, be said of Warren.

From Sonny......

Chick left Winnipeg to join St Catherine Teepees before crossing the big pond to play for the Nottingham Panthers. Chick wasn't a very tall man, but wide and stocky - with plenty of muscle on his body. His greatest asset was his marvellous shot which was always very low. The goalies had little chance as he could shoot on the move at high speed and with a lightning quick release while stickhandling. As said above, he was unsurpassed.

He was voted 'Sportsman of the Year', by the citizens of Nottingham, which was not all that surprising in itself. The icing on the cake, with regards to that award, was the competition that he beat to earn it. The other main contender was Tommy Lawton, England's star football centre-forward and a Notts County legend.

Chick now lives in Sevenoaks, Kent, with his wife. The last time I saw Chick was on an outing with my granddaughters to Windsor Safari Park a few years back. I bumped into him at a vending stall where we both stared at each other as we wondered if the person we were looking at was the person we thought it was. Time just seems to fly by, and the world really is a small place.

As for that young winger, John Rost, I suppose he didn't do too bad for himself!

No 5: Les Strongman

Les Strongman (right) about to score in a Panthers v. Sweden match (1952).

When the author first started watching ice hockey at Wembley in the mid-1960's, one of the Lions players who was instantly recognisable was Les Strongman. In those days helmets were not mandatory and most players chose not to wear one, but Les always wore white headgear. This was due to a fractured skull that he sustained in 1950, and while many thought then that his career was over, it was reported that the, *"rangy Winnipeg-born forward made a remarkable recovery and was soon back on the ice."*

Les played for Nottingham Panthers on their formation in 1946, and was a member of their English National League Championship winning teams of 1951 and 1954. He left in 1955 to play and coach for Zurich Schlitzer and returned the following season, only to play for rivals Wembley, where, once again, he won a Championship medal. In 1958 he returned to Panthers for a year before going abroad again, this time to Malmo in Sweden.

In 1963 he moved back to live in Nottingham but the Panthers and the National League were now defunct, so he didn't resume playing in Britain until Wembley Lions reformed in 1965. He continued to commute to play in the capital until the Lions finally folded in 1969.

When ice hockey returned to Lower Parliament Street in 1980, Les was one of the first to sign up - as coach only however - though he did play for the reformed side in a non-contact game against Baden Old Timers, a Canadian Air Force team. At the age of 56 and almost 35 years after his debut for the Panthers, Les scored 1+2 in a 14-5 victory.

Les was elected to the Hall of Fame in April 1987. He totalled 903 points in a 626 game career (515+388) and was nominated to the All-Star team seven times.

From Sonny......

Les Strongman was a fellow player - and now a friend I have known for 45 years. Les was a coaches dream; excellent attitude and ability. He was an absolute nightmare for the opposition.

He was a tireless backchecker, visionary playmaker and deadly goalscorer. Les was a tall player with long arms and legs. Once he got those legs in gear there was no chance of catching him.

He also had a brother called Bernie who played in the professional International and Western Hockey Leagues. Bernie was always high in the points table. Les said that his brother was better than him, but I still think that this was the only time he told me 'porkies'.

Les remained in Nottingham with his beautiful wife and family, and has been dedicated to the organisation and its supporters. Last time I spoke to him he was selling programmes inside the stadium. I hope to see him soon.

Les relaxes in the dressing-room, before a Wembley Lions v. Brighton Tigers match in 1967.

No 6: Bert & Tony Lemay

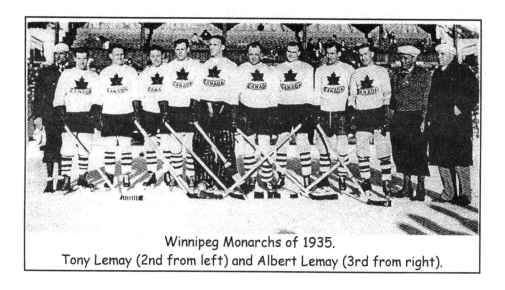

Winnipeg Monarchs of 1935.
Tony Lemay (2nd from left) and Albert Lemay (3rd from right).

I (the author) have a fascinating little paperback in my collection of ice hockey memorabilia. Written by Vince Leah and published in 1970 at the princely sum of $1.25, it is entitled '100 Years of Hockey in Manitoba', and though it may be questioned if it is pertinent to the British game, a quick look through the pages will tell you that since the day that the pioneering Sonny Rost left Winnipeg for London in 1934, many more great Manitoban hockey players have graced the game in this country.

Brothers Tony and Albert Lemay were from St. Boniface, and played for Winnipeg Monarchs when they successfully represented Canada in the 1935 World Championships at Davos, Switzerland. '100 Years' recalled that, *"Monarchs opened their world tournament play by defeating Great Britain 4-2. It was a tough struggle but the 'Peggers', sparked by Norm Yellowlees with two goals, prevailed at the end. Albert and Tony Lemay also scored one each, as they skated the British side into the ice as the battle wore on."*

After their success at international level, the brothers came to London to play for Wembley Lions, and Sonny Rost was once quoted as saying that, *"you won't see many better left-wingers than Albert Lemay."*

In a Lions v Monarchs programme from 1940, which was a double-header with a Canadian Expeditionary Force Challenge Match between Toronto Scottish and 2nd Royal Canadian Artillery Regiment, the programme editorial defends the criticism from some of the Canadian soldiers that British hockey was 'Kid-gloved'. It quotes Albert Lemay - by then back in Canada - as saying; *"We would like to have stayed at Wembley, settle down there. It's a great place to live, is England, and a great place to play hockey. The game is tougher in England. Sure enough you haven't got the high sticks and the charging over there; but they hand out some pretty stiff body checks and they play the game hard."*

From Sonny......

Hockey brothers Bert and Tony Lemay were in a class of their own. They had many offers from various teams, including one from Montreal Canadians of the NHL, but they decided to play top senior hockey instead.

They were excellent going forward with a trademark 'criss cross/scissors' play that left many defencemen in a daze, and the puck in the back of the net. On the right-wing with them was Alec Archer - also from Winnipeg. Alec played for the British Olympic team, and sure earned his gold medal. A tireless backchecker with the ability to score goals as well, he made it the perfect line.

The brothers loved to play the stock market and had a good business sense, which they used when they started a successful transport company. They were quoted as saying that British hockey was the highest paid and best in the World.

Wembley 1939.

Stapleford
Bert Lemay
Rheault
Stinchcombe
and Sonny
Rost.

No 7: Jo Jo Graboski

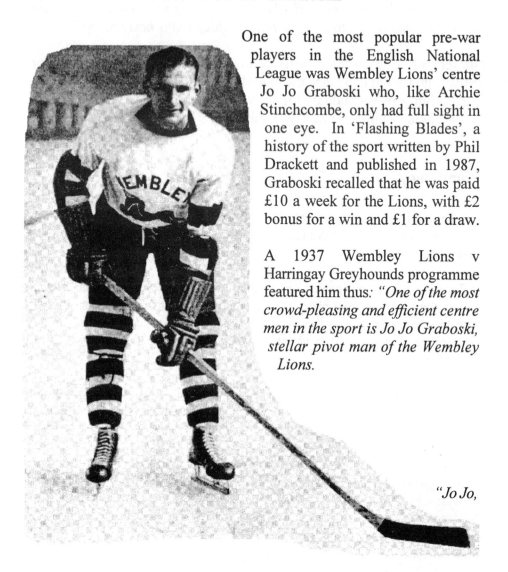

One of the most popular pre-war players in the English National League was Wembley Lions' centre Jo Jo Graboski who, like Archie Stinchcombe, only had full sight in one eye. In 'Flashing Blades', a history of the sport written by Phil Drackett and published in 1987, Graboski recalled that he was paid £10 a week for the Lions, with £2 bonus for a win and £1 for a draw.

A 1937 Wembley Lions v Harringay Greyhounds programme featured him thus: *"One of the most crowd-pleasing and efficient centre men in the sport is Jo Jo Graboski, stellar pivot man of the Wembley Lions.*

"Jo Jo,

unfortunately, sustained a broken nose in the series held in Toronto and has decided to stay over in Canada until the start of next season.

"A born comedian, Jo Jo has been one of the most popular players in the Wembley ranks with his fine sense of humour. Chief hobbies are sleeping and reading mail from Canada, from where he used to have an average of over five letters each delivery.

"Despite his severe handicap of playing with but one eye, Jo Jo is one of the most feared marksmen in the League. He is expected to be a married man before he returns to play for the Wembley Lions next season."

The series in Canada that is referred to, is a rare occasion when a senior British club ventured to the home of ice hockey. This unofficial World Cup round-robin between Sudbury Frood, Winnipeg Monarchs, Hershey Bears and Wembley Lions was won by Sudbury.

From Sonny ......

Well I remember the £10 a week days, but to put it into perspective you have to realise that cleaners at Wembley got £2 a week- with beer at 4p a pint, so we did pretty well.

Jo Jo was a very strong player, an excellent shot and almost immovable when he had the puck. He was always doing one arm pull-ups in the gym. He was unsurpassed at controlling the puck and the crowd used to gasp when he got it. Although he was one of the best individual players I've ever seen he wasn't much of a play-maker.

Jo Jo was funny with a very dry sense of humour. He never mixed very much with the other players, but we all liked and respected him none the less. He did strike up a friendship with Len Godin whom I still exchange letters with.

The tournament where he broke his nose was won by Sudbury Food - a team run by a mining company. There were about six of these places like Timmins, Conniston and North Bay. They would employ the players as miners as well so they received two wage packets but didn't usually work very much. Once the winter arrived in those days, there wasn't much to do in those places but watch or play hockey.

I have fond memories of Jo Jo, and would like to say that if he had two good eyes he would have played for Montreal Canadians when the NHL was only six teams.

No 8: Lou Bates

Lou Bates, as portrayed by a Prague cartoonist in 1934......

...... and with 'our Gracie' (Fields)

In 'Flashing Blades', Phil Drackett called Lou Bates 'Mr Ice Hockey' of the 1930's, and wrote that, *"of all the colourful players Wembley signed, none could match the charisma of the Lions' captain."* Phil continued that Lou *"had that extra something which makes the crowd flock to see a George Best, an Ian Botham, or a Muhammed Ali."*

Lou was so popular that he was featured on cigarette cards and in newspaper cartoons, as well as having his photograph taken with the celebrities of the day. In a March 1935 Lions programme, for example, he is pictured presenting a bouquet of flowers to Gracie Fields who, *"is at present engaged in the production of her new film, 'Look Up and Laugh'."*

Lou originally came to Europe on tour in 1933/34 with the Ottawa Shamrocks and stayed over to play in Paris for Français Volantes. The following season the Empire Pool was opened and Lou signed for Wembley Lions.

When elected to the - 'Hall of Fame' in 1950 (or 'Wall of Fame' as it was known then), the 'Ice Hockey World' wrote, *"the names of Bates and Wembley are synonymous. He led Lions to their first match back in 1934, and he was still associated with them as coach in 1947.*

"It is on record that the great days of Wembley teams were with Lou at the helm. Since Lou and Wembley came to the parting of the ways and the crowds roar of "Lou-oo-oo-oo!" has been silenced, there has been a void along the Great Ice Way."

An article in a Lions v Brighton Tigers programme from 1939 records: *"One member of the Lions team who is deserving of great credit in recent games is Lou Bates. Lou has been taking his place on the defence in all the recent important games despite a painful injury to his arm which has refused to yield to treatment. Lou suffered a blow on the muscles of his left arm and it has swollen to unbelievable size - but Lou refuses to step down."*

That particular night, however, Lou was scratched from the team sheet. One of the defenceman who had to cover for him in a 5-2 victory was Sonny Rost.

From Sonny ......

What can I say about my best friend Lou? He was a very fast skater, whose lone rushes from behind his own net were legendary. He would split a defence like butter. One of the best all round athletes that Ottawa ever produced. He was Canadian canoeing champion, played American Football for Ottawa, and had big offers from Boston Bruins of the NHL. His team mate - Bill Cowley - led the scoring, but Lou was reckoned to be better than him.

He was born in Ottawa, and went to one of the best colleges in Canada, Ashbury. One of his classmates was Ernie Ramus - who now sits on the BIHA. Christened John Louis Algenon McVicar Asquith Bates, his family had a Royal Crest and were distant relatives of the Prime Minister Lord Asquith.

Lou died about 12 years ago after living out his days at Wembley. Lou was a gentleman, and one of the best ambassadors hockey ever had. It was an honour to play with him.

No 9: Sandy Archer

The story goes that in his days as a coach, Sandy Archer once announced to his team: *"We are going to start from the beginning and discuss fundamentals."* A big defenceman sitting at the back called out, *"hey coach, what's a fundamental?"*

Alexander 'Sandy' Archer - a 'quiet thoughtful man' - was born in West Ham, London in May 1911, but was taken to Winnipeg, Manitoba as a three year-old. He returned to play for Wembley Lions, but his career was interrupted by the Second World War, and after an injury in 1945, he retired and took to coaching.

Wembley fans will remember him for being part of *"one of the most powerful lines in the history of British hockey"*, when he played right-wing for the Lemay brothers, while he was revered in the rest of the country for his part in helping Great Britain win the 1936 Olympic Gold Medal.

In 1993 the Writers' Association elected Sandy, in a one-off move along with all the other members of the successful Olympic squad, to the Hockey Hall of Fame. A 1939 Wembley Lions v Brighton Tigers programme editorial reported that *"the Sir Noel Curtis-Bennett Sportsman's Bowl has been won this year by Alex Archer, popular Lions' winger."*

The Supporters Club page endorses Sandy's selection with a number of letters from the fans. Supporter No: 10,970 - H. Cade - wrote *"In my opinion Alex Archer is one of the finest, hard-working, players in English ice hockey. Clean play must surely be Sandy's motto. The penalties he has received this season are very few indeed; and often he renders assistance to the opponent he has accidentally knocked over.*

"At backchecking Sandy has few equals. Stamina and speed are his two greatest assets, his stick handling is neat and effective, rarely disputes a referee's decision and is not subject to sudden changes of temperament."

Another supporter, Frances Beale, wrote: *"Popular? The fans never yell 'Wake up Archer.' It's always 'Good Old Archer.' I guess that means they like him."*

From Sonny......

Sandy Archer was a personal friend who, although born over here, learnt his hockey the hard way - in the open air rinks by the city of Winnipeg. He left Manitoba for Wembley and played for the Lions.

He fractured his skull playing against Sweden at Wembley, and was never the same again. They weren't even going to take him to hospital until his wife, who had some medical training, insisted. After that he won a Gold Medal at the Olympics, and was the GB Coach, Percy Nicklin's, favourite player.

Sandy coached Britain, Switzerland, Germany and Spain, learning the German and Spanish languages along the way.

He married, Doris Cutler - whose brother was the Lord Mayor of London. Although Sandy has been dead nearly 16 years, Doris is alive and well, running a successful homeopathy clinic in Axminster, Devon.

No 10: Archie Creighton

Yet another great 'Winnipegger' to grace the early days of British ice hockey was Archie Creighton, and there is an interesting photograph of him in the colours of the 1931 Elmwood Millionaires team, who were Junior hockey champions of Canada - the winners of the Memorial Cup.

He was also a member of the great 1935 Winnipeg Monarchs team, which included other future stars of the English circuit- Bert & Tony Lemay and Cam Shewan. Monarchs won the World Championship for Canada that year in Davos, Switzerland.

Creighton joined Harringay Racers when they were formed in the 1936/37 season, and was right-wing in their championship winning squad the following year. In the 1939/40 season he converted to defence with *"considerable success"*, and a March 1940 Racers-Streatham programme reported: *"There was never any question that Archie Creighton was a fine ice hockey player, but even his team-mates are amazed at the great job Archie is turning in on defence this year. As Pop Monson says: 'When Archie stops a play, he knows what to do with that puck. There is no man in English ice hockey so quick to see an opportunity and seize it."*

From Sonny......

Although we were mortal enemies on the ice, I was friendly with Archie off of it, and we would often share a beer after the game with another great friend of his - 'Pop' Monson.

I think that he must have had a trench dug along the barrier, because he patrolled up and down the wing like a mountie never losing his man on the backcheck. I think that the opposition wingers must have eventually given up the ghost. The defenceman on his side of the ice never had to worry about that man getting free.

Before coming to Britain, Archie played in Ottawa, Winnipeg, and then Flin Flon - a gold mining town north of Winnipeg. Farewell to another winger with wings.

No 11: Scottie Milne

For my sins, as well as being an ice hockey fan, I have followed the fortunes of Brentford Football Club through thick and thin, and from time to time connections are thrown up between the two. One recent connection is the Heath family. Dennis Heath - a tricky winger, was one of my first heroes when my Dad started to take me to the Griffin Park terraces in the late 1950's, while sons David and Steve both enjoyed careers as ice hockey players during the revival of the sport in the 1980's and 90's.

Perhaps one of the most tenuous connections between ice hockey and Brentford however is the fact that they both enjoyed their 'Golden Days' in the 1930's when between 1935 and 1938, while the crowds were flocking to Wembley, Harringay and Earls Court for ice hockey, the Bees enjoyed three consecutive top six placings in what is now the Premier League.

Wembley Lions and GB right-winger Alex Archer, was reported to have followed Brentford faithfully, and a January 1936 Wembley All Stars v National League All Stars programme has an article by 'Centre Ice' of the 'News of the World' who wrote: *"Football is the obsession of Archer and Milne. My telephone goes regularly at eleven o'clock every Saturday morning. Scottie is at the other end. 'Can you fix us for Brentford?' Or some other match."*

Ronald 'Scottie' Milne was brought up in Glasgow - adjacent to Crossmyloof ice rink- before emigrating to Canada as an eleven year old. When he returned it was to play football, and he signed for Glasgow

Rangers before moving to London in season 1934/35 where he swapped to ice hockey - joining Wembley but loaned out to Richmond Hawks. The following year he returned to Wembley Lions and in 1936/37 played back-up for Harringay.

Eventually Scottie decided to return to Scotland where he starred in the championship winning Perth Panthers team, but the connections with football are not lost as he also signed for the local Scottish League team, St Johnstone.

A March 1935 Wembley Lions v Richmond programme - the oldest in the Author's collection, shows Scottie in goal for Hawks in a 9-5 defeat. The programme doubles with a ladies international game between England and France. At number 8 for England in a 0-0 draw is Doris Heath. Who knows? Perhaps this is the reason why David and Steve have ice hockey instead of football in their blood.

From Sonny......

Scottie was a big strong man and a good football goalkeeper, but not truly outstanding. Who knows if he would have made pro soccer, but I think his first love was hockey.

At Wembley he was replaced by Art Childs and I don't think he ever forgave Lou Bates for the switch. Art Childs was back up goalie for the British Olympic team.

I visited Scottie in Vancouver, where he had a huge trophy room full of pictures and medals. Both hockey players and footballers adorned the walls.

He kept up his involvement with hockey and served as chief scout for New York Rangers in Western Canada. Unfortunately, Scottie is no longer with his wife Betty, a Scottish born lass and another great character.

No 12: George Beach

George Beach, nicknamed the 'Regina Peach', was born in Regina, Saskatchewan on 4th October 1926, and, according to his citation to the Hall of Fame in 1989, came to play for Wembley Lions in 1947. The Herald Ice Hockey Annual for 1968/69 however, claimed that he orig-inally played for Wembley Monarchs in 1948, and also recorded that *"he is one of the games most colourful characters, and 'comedian' of the Wembley team."*

It appears that George was in fact a member of the 1947 Lions squad, who he joined after attending the Chicago Blackhawks training camp and topped their scoring lists that year. He then alternated between Lions and Monarchs until 1954, when he tried his fortunes in Europe as player-coach. In 1959 he came back to play for Wembley and Southampton Vikings until his retirement in 1968.

In 1970/71 he returned briefly to play for the homeless Wembley Vets in the newly formed Southern League. He topped the scoring charts with 7 goals and 10 assists in four games as Vets finished third behind Sussex Senators and Altrincham Aces in a five team circuit. In 1975/76 George coached Great Britain in a disastrous World Championship and Pondus Cup campaign.

George won the Sportsman's Bowl on three occasions, and was voted to the All-Star team in 1950, 1951 and 1960. When selected in 1951 The Ice Hockey World Annual wrote: *"Player of the year was undoubtedly Monarch centreman George Beach."*

While George's goal tally is recorded as 608 in official competition, it was reported in 1968 that he was only the second player (after Chick Zamick) to reach 1,000 in all games. The landmark goal was scored against Fife Flyers on the 20th April, 1968. Michael Taub wrote in the Ice Hockey Herald Annual: *"He did it with his first serious effort, an angled shot which flashed past Fife's guest netminder, Roger Turner, in the sixth minute."*

Nearly there! George celebrates after scoring his 998th goal (Versus Glasgow Dynamos)

"The whole arena erupted into a mass of stamping and cheering as the large crowd showed their appreciation. George was besieged by back-slapping team-mates, and even the Fife players sportingly added their congratulations."

From Sonny ......

George performs some D.I.Y. in the dressing-room.

George Beach is one of my best friends, and was also a star centre. He had a high opinion of himself, and why not? In one season alone he won the scoring title of the Nat-ional League, Autumn Cup and the International League. He scored over 1,000 goals and won the Sir Noel Curtis Award three times, as well as meeting members of the royal family.

He was born in Regina, Sas-katchewan, and was asked by a scout to attend the Chicago Blackhawks training camp. He made the team, but was sent to their farm team, the Kansas City Pla-mors, who went on to win their league.

He was scouted for Wembley by Lou Bates, but the following season Lions were reorganised and I snapped him up for Monarchs - one of the best moves that I ever made - he always gave me 100% on the ice.

He is married to Jean, a lovely girl, and they have two sons. They now live in Eastcote, Middlesex. Aptly named the 'Regina Peach', George is a great star of the past.

No 13: Gordon Dailley

Despite being one of the outstanding stars of the pre-war English National League and a member of the British 1936 Olympic gold winning squad, I can find few references to Gordon Dailley in the programmes of that era in my possession.

Born in Canada, Dailley came to Britain in 1933 - working his passage on a cattle boat. He arrived before the large arenas at Wembley, Harringay and Earls Court had been built, and first played for Grosvenor House Canadians when they won the league championship in 1933/34.

When the Empire Pool opened for ice hockey, he moved out of the West End to North London and played for Wembley Canadians, Lions and Monarchs until the start of World War Two.

Despite his country of birth, he represented Great Britain in five World Championships - captaining his adopted nation in 1938 and 1939. Along with the other members of the 1936 Olympic Champions, Gordon was elected to the Hockey Hall of Fame in 1993.

Gordon died back in Canada aged 77 in May 1989 at Cambridge, Ontario. His obituary in the 1990/91 Ice Hockey Annual recorded that, "away from the ice, Gordon had a distinguished military career, reaching the rank of colonel in 1955 while serving with the UN peacekeeping forces in Korea."

From Sonny......

Gordon gives advice to sixteen year-old Arthur Green, in 1939.

Born and educated in Winnipeg, Gordon was a bit of a scholar and received higher than average grades from school. He played the first year at Wembley on a high scoring line with Edgar J. Murphy at Centre and Bobby Walton on the Right Wing.

Gordon was big and strong - and not someone to try and intimidate. If you tried you would have to watch yourself, while his line-mates were the sharpshooters. Walton went back to North America where he played in the professional American Hockey League for Pittsburgh Hornets, topping the scoring charts and getting selected for the All Star First Team.

Gordon became a Colonel in the Canadian Army, and then the military attache for Canada in Romania. He went back to Ottawa to settle down, but tragedy struck and his son was drowned when he fell into a storm drain and was washed away. A cruel blow to a person who had led a distinguished life.

No 14: Art Child

SUPPLEMENT TO RADIO TIMES, JANUARY 22, 1937

RADIO TIMES

TELEVISION

SUPPLEMENT

PROGRAMMES FROM JANUARY 25 TO 30

ICE-HOCKEY

ART CHILD, goalminder, and
JIMMY CHAPPELL, forward,
two members of the British Olympic team, are to be televised on Tuesday

Front page news!

Wembley Lions goalie Arthur 'Art' Child won a gold medal with Great
Britain's 1936 Olympic squad - but never took to the ice, playing second
fiddle to the outstanding Jimmy Foster of Richmond Hawks. He led a
colourful life before during and after his hockey career which peaked when
he became a Member of the Canadian Parliament.

A 1936 Wembley programme featured him in an article which included: *"Art Child has crowded quite a lot into his short life since he was born in East Ham 23 years ago. He lived in London until just after the [first world] war, when he went to Canada with his father, mother and brother."*

While at school in Toronto he learned to play ice hockey; at the age of 19 he hoboed his way across Canada and back; shortly after he took a diploma for scientific bakery and had even grown a beard at an age when most men are still trying to encourage a toothbrush moustache!

It is very likely that Art could write a book about his experiences as a hobo. After he had travelled some 9,000 miles in six weeks by jumping freight trains and tramping the roads, he certainly did appreciate his home. He stood in bread lines, visited soup kitchens or begged his food wherever he could. The whole journey cost him 30 shillings (£1.50).

What was the big idea in undertaking this definitely uncomfortable journey? *"Oh for experience"*, was the disconcerting reply. *"In any case, I have got the travel bug badly, which is why I came over to England this winter. I took a chance that' someone - preferably Wembley - would give me the opportunity to play hockey."*

From Sonny......

Art was one of the many babies born after the lst World War to British parents who then settled in Canada. He made his own way over to Britain without a contract but was immediately signed by Wembley Lions coach, Lou Bates, to replace the *"average Scotty Milne"* in the net.

When Art played for the Lions, he vowed not to shave until he had a shut-out, which earned him the nickname 'Beaver'. I remember the beard lasting three or four months before he kept his first clean sheet.

He was selected to play for Great Britain, but had the misfortune to back up one of the best goalies of the day anywhere in the world - Jimmy Foster. Although he didn't get any starts (in the Olympics), I know he would have done a superb job because he is one of the best goalies that I've seen.

When Art returned to Canada, he played in the Ontario senior league where he was an All-Star before entering politics and becoming the MP for Hamilton. These days he runs a successful consultancy firm in Hamilton.

1 last saw him almost a decade ago when I was visiting my brother Wally, and we got together with Art, Lou Bates and Len Godin. It was a great time, and 'Beaver' and myself still exchange cards from time to time.

I remember Art being very fair all the time, a big strong man who never drank or smoked. He would challenge the other players to a contest for Cokes at the end of practise - one shot, score or miss. He would end up with enough Coke to last the whole season.

1935: The Wembley Canadians remove the beard
of Lions' goal-minder Art Childs.

No 15: Paul Rheault

Paul Rheault - part of the 1937 Winnipeg Monarchs Junior hockey champions team.

Many of the pre-war National League teams iced French-Canadian players, who were often considered talented and entertaining but volatile - much in the same way as these days Eric Cantona is in Soccer, or the French Rugby Union team is in their code.

The numbers reached a peak in season 1936/37, when Rapide de Paris and Français Volantes were invited to play in the English National League. Unfortunately both teams struggled financially, and had to move their operations to England, finishing the campaign as Manchester Rapids and Southampton Vikings.

Paul Rheault played for Wembley Lions before moving to Kirkcaldy to star in the last Fife Flyers team before hostilities started with Germany. A January 1939 Wem-bley Lions v Earls Court Rangers programme recorded: *"Paul Rheault, speedy left wing star of the Wembley Lions is rapidly establishing himself as a serious rival to his fellow French Canadian, Frank Cadorette, for 'quaint sayings' in and around the dressing rooms."*

"Paul's latest utterance was one that caused great amusement to his team mates. Just as the Lions were about to go on the ice for their match with their rink rivals, the Monarchs, Paul was heard to say: "Remember, you guys, we will have to 'contemplate' on backchecking if we hope to stop these Monarchs!"

"Rheault's play has been one of the bright spots during the long spell of ill fortune which has followed the National Tournament winners, and his knack of being in the right spot for loose pucks is proved by the goal scoring statistics which show the fiery young winger among the leaders."

At the time of the programme going to press, Lions and Rangers were equal bottom of the National League, and neither cause was improved when they shared the spoils with a 3-3 tie. Alex Archer (2) and Red Stapleford scored for the Lions while Jack Forsey (2) and Jerry Brown hit the mark for Rangers. Rheault got an assist while Sonny Rost also got on the scoresheet with one of Lions' five minor penalties. Both teams improved their league positions to finish second and third respectively.

From Sonny ......

Another classy player born in Winnipeg, Paul played for a team called Winnipeg Monarchs and helped them to win the Memorial Cup in 1935 and 1937. The first line in 1937 - Alfie Pike, Dick Kowcinak and Johnny McCreedy - went to the NHL and starred for many seasons.

Paul, while playing in Britain, was always a top scorer with a very hard snap shot about 10 inches off the ice. Around the net he always seemed to have eyes in the back of his head.

Unfortunately he had 'off-ice' problems, and was considered a bit of a playboy. I would have taken his voting rights away from him if I could!

We once played against Harringay for the league title, and he arrived under the influence. He cost us the championship and a lot of money. He went into hiding for three days after that as 'Sonny the Assassin' was hunting him down. I had him deported north of Watford. What a waste of talent!

Footnote:
In season 1938/39, Harringay Greyhounds pipped Wembley Lions to the English National League title by a solitary point. Lions met Greyhounds at the Empire Pool on Saturday 15th April 1939 - the last day of the campaign.

No: 16 Percy Nicklin

Before coming to England in 1935, Percy Nicklin coached Moncton Hawks to two Allan Cup championships. His career in the UK began with Richmond Hawks, who he steered to runners-up in the inaugural English National League - losing out to Wembley Lions on goal average.

In 1936 Nicklin achieved his greatest success. He and the BIHA secretary Bunny Ahearne travelled across the Atlantic to find Canadian stars who qualified by birth to play for Great Britain. This resulted in the almost impossible happening - Great Britain winning the Olympic, World and European Championships.

Percy then moved to the newly opened arena at Harringay, where he served as coach and later as rink manager until it closed down twenty-two years later. He died in the early 1970's and was elected to the Hall of Fame in 1988. At the time Phil Drackett - Editor of "Ice Hockey World" - collected his scroll as no surviving relatives could be found, but it was later sent on to his daughter Alma who was found to be living in Florida.

Percy Nicklin,
Harringay Greyhounds Coach

In a November 1936 Harringay Greyhounds programme, where rather ironically the opposition was Richmond Hawks, Louis Mckenna - a Canadian ice hockey journalist wrote: *"Harringay were wise in securing the services of Nicklin. They wanted and secured the best coach available for their magnificent new Arena. Nicklin set out to collect two powerful teams. He has them."*

In that season's English National League only Wembley Lions finished above the two Harringay clubs, with Racers beating Greyhounds to the runners-up spot by four points in a forty game schedule. Racers did win two trophies that year however - the Coronation Cup and the London Cup.

From Sonny......

Percy Nicklin was a very good friend and a giant amongst coaches and managers. He led the Great Britain team - which everyone knows won a gold medal in 1936. That was a feat to believe, and I think it will take a long time to emulate. If you played for 'Nick' you had to be a tireless backchecker, and never let your man escape.

Percy never got over the tragic loss of his son Jeff who was a Captain in the Canadian parachute regiment and played football for the Blue Bombers. During World War Two he landed over Belgium and was shot dead by a German sniper while hanging from a tree.

Although 'Nick' won a lot of trophies in his time it never made up for this loss. Harringay fans will never forget him and neither will I.

Percy Nicklin - Great Britain Coach,
with (left) Bob Bowman, Canadian commentator.

No 17: 'Duke' Campbell

Duke Campbell - Harringay Racers

Keith William 'Duke' Campbell - like Sonny Rost - was another great hockey player who had his career interrupted by World War Two. In the 1950/51 'Ice Hockey World Annual', it was noted that Duke's, *"remarkable career goes back fifteen years in English hockey and has just been climaxed by his appointment as player-coach to Earls Court Rangers. In that fifteen years Duke has played over 500 consecutive games and has never missed one encounter in which his team has been engaged. This, apart from war-time exhibition games."*

The earliest programme in the Author's collection where Duke can be found listed as playing, is a January 1936 Challenge match at the Empire Pool between a combined Wembley Canadians and Lions team against a National League All-Stars squad. Campbell is listed as right-wing for the All-Stars, and was at that time playing for Richmond Hawks, his first English club after crossing the Atlantic from Moncton.

He moved to Harringay when the Arena opened, and lead the Greyhounds to the league championship in 1940. He briefly played for Brighton before moving back to Harringay to play for the Racers - a move that upset many 'Hounds supporters. He completed a notable double by captaining Racers to the league title in 1949, before taking charge at Earls Court.

In 1948, Duke Campbell was the first person to be elected to the British Hockey Wall of Fame. At the time it was noted that, *"Canada has a 'Hall of Fame' at Kingston, Ontario, but as yet, we have not aspired to erecting a special building, so for the present a 'Wall' it is."* Almost half a century on we still don't have a building, but these days our heroes are now elected to the 'Hall of Fame'.

From Sonny......

Duke was born in Winnipeg, and played top senior hockey there. A stylish skater and a very fast Left or Right Winger, he was a good goal scorer and a tireless backchecker.

He played most of his hockey at Harringay, and went from Greyhounds to Racers where he became the player-coach. He dropped back into defence - a position he excelled in. He made most All-Star teams, and I think his nickname name should have been 'King' not 'Duke' Campbell.

He was the darling of the Harringay supporters, but sadly passed away a few years ago in Winnipeg. This was a personal loss to me as he was a very good friend. Adios Duke.

Duke Campbell
Richmond Hawks

No 18: Robert J 'Bobby' Giddens

*Bobby Giddens
Player-coach
of 1934/35
National League
Champions
Streatham*

Bobby Giddens was born in Ottawa, Ontario, on 15th March 1906, and originally came to Europe to play in Paris before moving to Streatham as player-coach in 1934. When Earls Court opened in 1935, Giddens moved from South London to the West End and took charge of one of their teams - Kensington Corinthians.

At around the same time he had founded a weekly newspaper - the 'Ice Hockey World' - which in its heyday (depending on various sources) had a circulation of between 35,000 and 50,000. Unfortunately Corinthians had a struggling team, and the conflicting pressures of being player, coach and journalist eventually lead to a fracas with a 'senior Earls Court official', and Giddens resigned as coach. For a short while he played for their sister team, Earls Court Rangers, but eventually he retired to concentrate on the newspaper.

Giddens versatility did not end there however, and when there was a shortage of referees at the onset of World War Two he volunteered to help out. Phil Drackett, Assistant Editor of 'The World' once recalled that, *"he was a good editor but a bad referee."*

In December 1952, Giddens and Drackett selected an All-Star team which lost 2-1 to Wembley Lions in a match attended by HRH The Duke of Edinburgh.

Giddens' also published nine 'Ice Hockey World Annuals' between 1947 and 1955 and wrote a book, 'Ice Hockey - the International Game', which was originally published in 1950 and reprinted in 1958. He founded the original British Ice Hockey Wall of Fame in 1948, and was elected to the Hall of Fame (as it is now known) in 1986. He died in London on 12th October 1963 after a long illness. At the time there was no league hockey being played in Britain, but he always believed that it would one day, once again, be a major sport in this country.

In his book, Giddens wrote: *"there should be enough signposts along the way to show that ice hockey is fundamentally a sound game, a good sport and a colourful spectacle which if promoted with vision, enthusiasm and sincerity could take its place proudly and without apology beside Football, Rugby and Cricket."*

From Sonny......

Bobby was from Ottawa, and a 'Capital City Boy'. His father was the Secretary for the Prime Minister of Canada, Mckenzie King. Bobby, as we called him, was a very good friend of Lou Bates.

Bobby went to Harvard University, and became the first Canadian to captain their hockey team - a big honour. An ambitious business man who founded the 'Ice Hockey World', a very good hockey paper with dedicated readers.

He had a brother - 'Babe' who came over in the early 1930's. 'Babe' was a first rate musician who played for the top bands.

Bobby was a good player, and a great unbiased editor for the 'World' for 20 years.

No 19: Bob Cornforth

Bob Cornforth receives a commemorative medalion from
H.R.H. the Duke of Edinburgh, following a charity game in December 1952

When Wembley Lions finished fifth of six teams and 17 points adrift of winners Streatham in the 1952 English Autumn Cup, there was little sign that they were about to embark on their first National League Championship success for fifteen years.

The league triumph was due in no small part to their defence, and, according to the 'Ice Hockey World Annual', *"the goalminding of Bob Cornforth was often an inspiration to his team-mates as was the sterling defence work of veteran Sonny Rost who shed the years along with his moustache and crash helmet."* The 'World' added , *"a good-looking, twenty-years-young Montrealer stood between the pipes for Wembley Lions during 1951 -52. and turned out to be a major cog in the machine which won the Championship."*

Bob Cornforth, rookie netman on his first visit to England, was voted by Wembley fans as their favourite player and selected by the experts as the All-Star 'B' Team goalminder. In point of fact he headed the goalminders' averages for the National League with a shots-per-goal figure over a whole point better than that of Earl Betker, the Streatham man who was voted to the 'A' team."

Cornforth also conceded 118 goals, better than any other goalie apart from Brighton's Gib Hutchinson who only conceded 114 - but he also played five less games so it seems a bit unfair that the Lions 'stopper' did not get selected to the 'A' Team.

Cornforth was born in Montreal on June 24th, 1931, and played all of his hockey in the Montreal Royals organisation from 12 years old to junior 'A', before crossing the Atlantic Ocean to make a name for himself in North London.

A photograph in the 1952/3 'Ice Hockey World Annual' has the headlines 'Supporters Laud Popular Wembley Netman', and underneath is written, *"Bob Cornforth, rookie goalie for league champions Wembley Lions, was honoured by supporters who banded together to buy him a Parker '51' pen and pencil set. That's Bob, hoisted upon the shoulders of his admiring fans and clutching the Sportsman Bowl, presented each season to Wembley's most valuable player."*

From Sonny ......

'Corny' we called him, but he sure didn't play corny. I played in front of him on defence, and any shots that did get by me, I knew I didn't have to even look back, because it wasn't going in.

He was a real 'greenhorn' when he arrived, but after a month or so me and the other older boys had turned him into a real mature English gent. He was a favourite with the fans - especially the ladies. There was always girls waiting for him outside the dressing room screaming for autographs.

When he went back to Canada, he studied physiotherapy in Montreal. He then became the physio' for the Montreal Canadians. He now has a successful practice in the city and lives pretty well. 'Corny' was a big part of our championship season.

No 20: Walter Rost

In the last 60 years or so the Rost family have made a massive contribution to British ice hockey. Sonny retired after a glorious career with Wembley when the first British League collapsed in 1960, but his son John was already making a name for himself and, like his Dad, was eventually elected to the Hall of Fame after playing for Brighton, Altrincham, Wembley and Streatham.

Walter Rost
December 1937

Warren became the third generation to play at Wembley when he captained Streatham Scorpions to a 7-0 victory over Fife Flames in the 1986 British Junior Final. Since then he has played in the British League for Streatham, Ayr and Slough.

A fourth Rost has also appeared at Wembley. Walter Rost, Sonny's brother, played for Wembley Canadians and Southampton Vikings in the pre-War English National League.

A December 1937 Wembley programme featured him thus: *"The younger of the Rost 'Brother Act' now playing at the Empire pool. One of the fastest skaters in the National League and a tenacious backchecker, Walter is an ideal defensive wing.*

"Though small of stature, he is seldom the victim of a bodycheck, being very tricky around the goal area. Throughout the summer months Walter is a keen follower of baseball and golf, being equally efficient on the diamonds and links as he is on the ice.

"Is playing his second year in England, and is one of the most improved players in the country. Like his brother 'Sonny', he enjoys a practical joke and is Jack Milford's chief aide in the latter's many pranks on his mates."

From Sonny ......

My brother Wally is two years younger than me, and learnt all of his hockey in Winnipeg. He was 'imported' to a small town called Poplar Point in Ontario to play in a team packed with great stars. These included some excellent NHL prospects led by 'Black Jack' Stewart who went on to play for the Chicago Blackhawks and the NHL All-Stars.

After reaching the Junior play-offs with Poplar Point he made the journey to London and played at Wembley. He was a clean player and a fast skater - not like his big brother!

He had two successful seasons with Wembley, before returning to Canada to play for the St Catherines Tee Pees and got a try-out for the Montreal Canadians. He used to live with Alec Archer, and although they were fairly different people they got on great.

Unfortunately he was injured and broke his back against the boards, spending a long time in hospital. General Motors sponsored the team and trained him to be a toolmaker. He then worked for them until he retired. He was a first class tradesman, working in the big car plant in St Catherines.

I still visit Wally once a year, and like me he is in good health. He has two children - a boy and a girl. His daughter Pat is a 'gold level' figure skater and now a first class judge.

No 21: Jimmy Haggarty

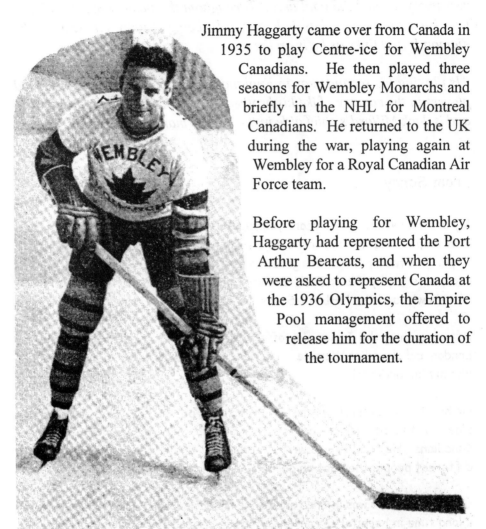

Jimmy Haggarty came over from Canada in 1935 to play Centre-ice for Wembley Canadians. He then played three seasons for Wembley Monarchs and briefly in the NHL for Montreal Canadians. He returned to the UK during the war, playing again at Wembley for a Royal Canadian Air Force team.

Before playing for Wembley, Haggarty had represented the Port Arthur Bearcats, and when they were asked to represent Canada at the 1936 Olympics, the Empire Pool management offered to release him for the duration of the tournament.

Fellow Wembley stars Art Child, Bob Wyman, Gordon Dailley, Alex Archer and Jack Kilpatrick opposed Haggarty in the victorious GB squad as Canada failed for the first time in Olympic history to win the gold medal.

A 1937 Wembley programme feature on Haggarty recorded that he was, *"one of the deadliest 'snipers' in the sport. A leading goal-getter for every team he has played for since he was a star in the 'midget' ranks in Canada. The shyest player in the country.*

Is called 'Blushing Jimmy' by his team-mates. Is an all-round athlete, especially keen on swimming, baseball, lawn tennis and table tennis. Chief hobbies are motoring and attending first night performances."

In his book 'Vendetta On Ice', Phil Drackett remembered that Haggarty, *"was a gentleman on and off the ice and won the first Curtis-Bennett Bowl for good sportsmanship in 1938. He was also a graphic illustration of the type of player who could do a good job without spending half his time in the penalty box."*

From Sonny......

Known as 'Gentleman Jim' he was an outstanding Centre who was always high in the goal scoring charts. He had an unstoppable shot from close quarters.

Jimmy was born in Port Arthur, now known as Lake Head and on the shore of the massive Lake Superior. He played his junior hockey for the Port Arthur Bear Cats, who met our team - Kenora Thistles - in Winnipeg for the Manitoba Junior Championships. They beat us 5-4 and Jimmy scored a hat -trick.

He declined NHL try-outs, and came over here to Wembley where we became great friends. Jimmy was selected to represent Canada in the 1936 Olympics along with some other Wembley players. He also represented Canada in Athletics at the Summer Olympics - though I cannot remember which event - Pole Vault I think.

Jimmy now lives in Montreal and is enjoying his retirement.

No 22: John Murray

Wembley Lions Player-coach

John Murray was born in 1924, and has spent much of his life involved in British ice hockey. He played in the pre-war Wembley junior set up before becoming a fully-fledged Lion after hostilities ended, though he was to enjoy more ice time with their reserve squad - Wembley Terriers.

When Lions folded along with the original British League in 1960, Murray went south with several other Wembley stars to play for Southampton Vikings, and when they also folded in 1963, Johnny returned to the Empire Pool to be player-coach of the reorganised non-league Wembley Lions.

He eventually retired at the end of the 1967/68 season, though he coached Lions in the next campaign, their last, when John Rost replaced him in the no.7 shirt. The 1968/69 Herald Ice Hockey Annual records that he played his first game for Lions as a 14 year-old in the 1938/39 season, though in the few programmes I have from that season, I can only find his name in the 'A' Team squad of a Junior League Trial Match.

The Herald Annual went on to recall that John represented Great Britain in *"Three successive Olympics, and numerous World and European championships. In fact, Murray captained Great Britain in eight World championships, one Olympic Games, and the European Championships at Liege in 1961."*

John represented the sport for a while on the International Olympic Committee. He has served on the BIHA council for more than 30 years, and was made a vice-president in 1982. In March 1996, he was inducted to the British Ice Hockey Hall of Fame.

From Sonny......

Wembley born John made the grade in the Canadian dominated National League. My impression of him was 'Brains before brawn John'. He was a dangerous man around goal and got his share of points.

He is married to Pam, a top class ballet dancer and a professional tutor, and they have two sons who are doing well. John and Pam spent their honeymoon on tour with Wembley Lions in Finland and Sweden. Imagine a lady on a bus loaded with hockey players, playing poker and gross language. I thought it might be a disaster, but when the trip was over the team gave Pam a standing ovation.

I played John at Centre, with wingers Mal Davidson and 'Lefty' Wilmott who never lost a battle in the corners. John led the team in scoring. There was no better person to represent his country abroad in tournaments and the Olympics. He has never left the hockey scene, and is now a vice-president of the BIHA. We are lucky to have him as a personal pal, to still be great friends, and we are always in touch.

John Murray in action, May 1964.

No 23: Frankie Leblanc

1937/38 Wembley Monarchs - National League Runners-up
Third from left - Frankie Leblanc, with Walter Rost on his right,
and Gordon Dailley second from right.

French-Canadian Frankie Leblanc came from Quebec and played for Montreal Royals and Moncton Hawks before coming to London to play for Queen's in the days before big-time hockey had hit England. The Queen's Ice Club was - and still is - based in Queensway, West London, and was not really suitable for the sport. The rink was long and narrow at 214 feet by 65, and could only accommodate around 1,000 spectators.

In a 1947 'Ice Hockey World', Al Hunt recalled that, *"many present day hockey fans don't associate the Bayswater rink with the puck and stick game but, believe me, Queen's has a hockey record which is truly a fine one. A treasured possession of manager G. Hales is a large bronze plaque awarded to Queen's in 1934 as Inter-European Champions. Among those on the successful team were that great stick-handler, the late Frankie Leblanc, and former Harringay Racer star, Archie Creighton."*

Leblanc went on to play for Wembley Canadians and Monarchs before being killed in a hunting accident. In 'Flashing Blades', Phil Drackett wrote that, *"it was worth the admission charge to see a man like Leblanc, a dipsey-doodle type of player who would show the puck to a defender and then dance away, ice hockey's version of football's Stanley Matthews."*

A column written by 'Icicle', in a 1937 Wembley programme observed that, *"a prominent factor in recent sterling performances of the Wembley Monarchs is the improved play of their alternate line.*

"Leading the trio is one of the most colourful ice hockey stars in the country Frankie Leblanc - noted for amazing stickhandling and worrying tactics around the goal area. With Leblanc distributing the puck to his wings the 'pony line' of the Regals, consisting of Walter Rost, Frankie Cadorette and Sammy Gigliotti, has blossomed into one of the most dangerous trios in the league.

"Leblanc at the start of the season was inclined to be selfish, a fault common to all fine stickhandlers, but the pestiferous centre is now making himself doubly valuable by passing the puck whenever he sees an opportunity of goal."

From Sonny ......

I played with Frank at Wembley and against him when he was at Harringay, and he was one of the best individual players that I have ever seen. Unfortunately he starved his forwards, and one reason not mentioned above was that he was deaf. His team-mates would shout and he just didn't hear them.

When he was in close on a goaltender, he would leave them spinning with machine gun like stickhandling. Really amazing to watch, in those days you had to be four feet from the barrier before you could be checked.

Unfortunately he had a fatal accident while duck-shooting with a friend. They were sharing a boat and his friend shouted for him to stay down. Frankie didn't hear the warning and took the full force of the blast in his upper body.

It turned into a double tragedy because his friend never forgave himself, and had a breakdown coming to terms with the incident. A tragic end to a nice guy and a great player.

Sonny Rost

(Top) A Rost Trio! (Left) Sonny, (middle) grandson Warren and (right) son John. (Above) Sonny in action against Nottingham Panthers in 1951, and (right) on the ice in 1947.

Chick
Zamick

(Top) In typical stance, when
with Nottingham Panthers,
and (left) in 1963, as a
Wembley Lions player.

Les Strongman

(Above) 1950 - with Nottingham Panthers.
(Below) Scoring for Wembley Lions in 1966
(third from left), on the far left George Beach
celebrates the goal.

(Above) Lou pictured back in 1936, and, (below) sharing memories with fellow Wembley idol, George Beach, in 1967.

Lou
Bates

Archie Creighton (left), with the 'Elmwood Millionaires', in 1931.

George Beach (above), celebrates after scoring his 1,000th goal, versus Fife Flyers in April 1968....

(below) with TV star Rosemary Leach and Lions' player coach Johnny Murray in November 1966.

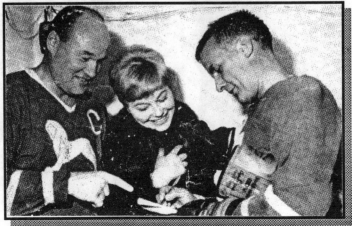

Duke Campbell
In 1947, with
Harringay Racers.

Bob Giddens
In 1935,
he launched
'Ice Hockey World'.

Johnny Murray
Wembley Terriers coach,
1951/52.

Sandy Archer
1946/47 coach
of Nottingham Panthers.

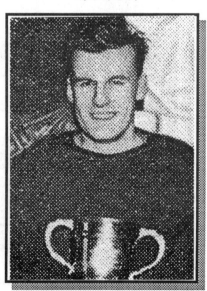

✳ The Stars and some of their teams ✳

WEMBLEY LIONS: 1934/35.
(Back) Westaway, Head, Bert Forsyth, Murphy, **Lou Bates,** Peacock.
(Front) **Gordon Dailley,** Grace, Cosby, Ted Jackson, S.Jackson, J.Forsyth, Walton, Coulter

GREAT BRITAIN: 1936
(Back) Chappell, **Archie Stinchcombe, Sandy Archer, Gordon, Dailley,**
Percy Nicklin (Coach), Kilpatrick, Erhardt, Coward, Davey.
(Front) Borland, **Art Child,** Foster, Brenchley.

STREATHAM: 1936/37.

HARINGAY GREYHOUNDS: 1937/38.
(Back) **Percy Nicklin, Duke Campbell,** *Hefferman, Jones, Adolph, McAndrew, Nicholson, Taylor, Clarke*
(Front) Shack, Brunning, Foster, Beaton, Cheyne.

HARRINGAY RACERS: 1937/38.
(Back) Whitelaw, Arnott, Pearson, **Percy Nicklin** *(coach), Taylor,*
Major Mackenzie, **Bert Peer, Archie Creighton,** *Latoski, Clarke*
(Front) Keating, Goldie, Heximer, **Wally Monson,** *Burrage, Hogarth.*

NOTTINGHAM PANTHERS: 1950/51.
(Back) Casey, Kieran, **Les Strongman,** *Moulden, Ringer, Allen,*
McDonald, Woods, **Chick Zamick,** *Cragg*
(Seated) Pyryhors, Johnson, Watson. (Kneeling) James, Ware, **Archie Stinchcombe.**

ALL-STARS: October 1964
(Back) 'Wally', O'Brien, Dobbyn, McNeil, Bremner, Whitehead, Haines, **George Beach.**
(Front) Whittal, **Sonny Rost,** *Thomas,* **Johnny Murray,** *Devereaux.*

WEMBLEY LIONS: 1968/69
(Back) Devereaux, Shepherd, **Les Strongman,** *Whitehead, Cook, Hodgins*
(Back) Imrie, John Rost, Thomas, **George Beach,** *Fresher.*

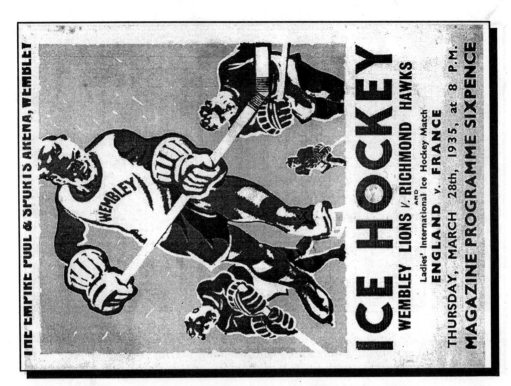

ICE HOCKEY

THE EMPIRE POOL & SPORTS ARENA, WEMBLEY

WEMBLEY LIONS v. RICHMOND HAWKS

AND

Ladies' International Ice Hockey Match

ENGLAND v. FRANCE

THURSDAY, MARCH 28th, 1935, at 8 P.M.

MAGAZINE PROGRAMME SIXPENCE

PROGRAMMES FROM THE GOLDEN AGE

EMPIRE POOL

& SPORTS ARENA

WEMBLEY

WEMBLEY CANADIANS

v.

RICHMOND HAWKS

SATURDAY, MARCH 7th, 1936, at 8 p.m.

MAGAZINE PROGRAMME SIXPENCE

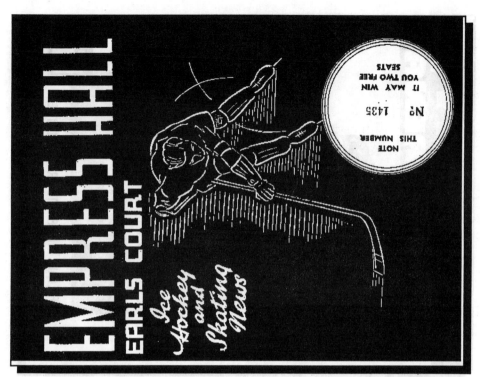

(Programme versus Brighton Tigers - 5 March 1938)

(Programme - Harringay Racers v. Streatham - 2nd March 1940)

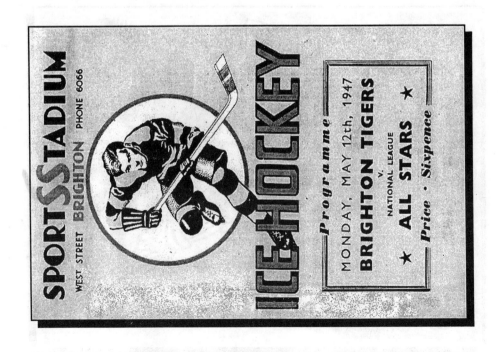

Sports-Drome
RICHMOND ICE RINK

INTER-VARSITY
ICE HOCKEY MATCH

★

OXFORD
VERSUS
CAMBRIDGE

★

The Trophy will be presented to the Winning Team by
AIR VICE MARSHAL SIR VICTOR TAIT, K.B.E.
(Vice-President British Ice Hockey Association)

FRIDAY
15th FEBRUARY
1952

SPORTS-DROME
(RICHMOND ICE RINK)
RICHMOND BRIDGE
E. TWICKENHAM
Phone POPesgrove 3646

Streatham Ice Rink
Telephone:
STREATHAM
7861-2-3
1233

PROGRAMME
6d.

WEDNESDAY
OCTOBER
7th
1953
●
AUTUMN CUP

ICE HOCKEY

★ STREATHAM v. NOTTINGHAM PANTHERS

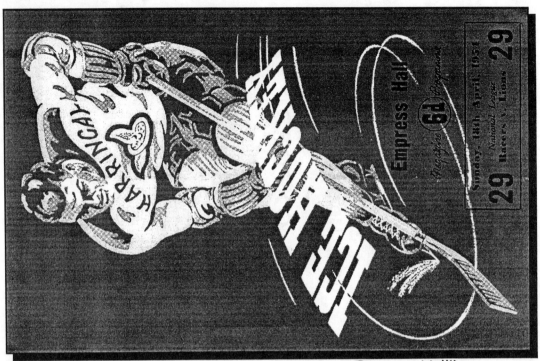

(A Haringay Racers 'Home' game - at Empress Hall!)

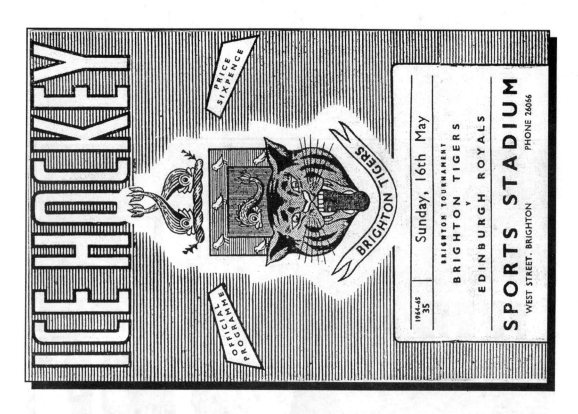

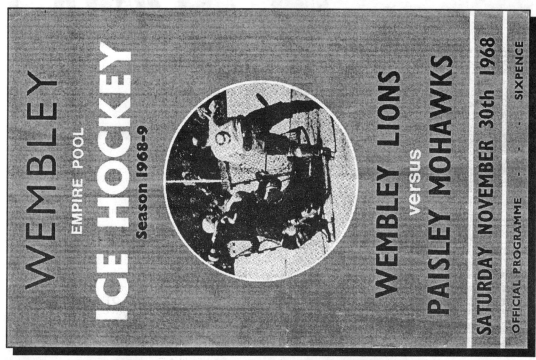

(Wembley Lions last ever game at the Empire Pool)

And Finally........

The Beginning, at The End!

Where it all began in July 1934.
The opening of the Empire Pool, Wembley, by The Duke of Gloucester.